GOOD MANNERS in PUBLIC

by Ann Ingalls • illustrated by Ronnie Rooney

The Child's World

Published by The Child's World®
1980 Lookout Drive • Mankato, MN 56003-1705
800-599-READ • www.childsworld.com

Acknowledgments
The Child's World®: Mary Berendes, Publishing Director
The Design Lab: Design and production
Red Line Editorial: Editorial direction

ISBN 9781614732266
LCCN 2012932470

Printed in the United States of America
Mankato, MN
July 2012
PA02126

ABOUT THE AUTHOR

Ann Ingalls writes books, short stories and poems for people of all ages as well as resource materials for parents and teachers. She was a teacher for many years and enjoys working with children. When she is not writing, she enjoys spending time with her family and friends, traveling, reading, knitting, and playing with her cats.

ABOUT THE ILLUSTRATOR

Ronnie Rooney took art classes constantly as a child. She was always drawing and painting at her mom's kitchen table. She got her BFA in painting from the University of Massachusetts at Amherst and her MFA in Illustration from Savannah College of Art and Design in Savannah, Georgia. She now lives and works in Fort Lewis, Washington. Her plan is to pass her love of art and sports on to her two young children.

CONTENTS

Manners in Public

It is time to leave the house! Now you are in public space. A public space is a space that you share with other people. Parks, stores, and libraries are public spaces. Movie theaters and restaurants are public spaces, too. Many spaces are public.

You need to be **polite** in public. Some people are not, though. Have you gone to the movies and sat next to some loud people? Did they use bad language or talk on a cell phone? How did you feel?

They did not **respect** your space. You can respect other people in public. Keep your music or your voice down. Use good words, too. Tossing around bad words is like tossing garbage. After a while, it stinks.

Rules of the Road

It is hard to walk on a crowded sidewalk or in a hallway. You should stay to the right when you walk. Pass others on the left side. Don't be a hog. Leave some space for others. You should think about who is stuck behind you. If you know someone wants to pass, move to the side. And do not spit on the street. No one wants to get splashed in the face!

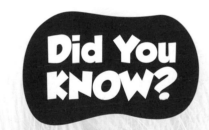

Did You KNOW?

In Australia it is really bad manners to spit. It is even against the law to do so in public!

Using Umbrellas

On rainy days, many people carry umbrellas. If you share an umbrella, let the taller person hold it. If you meet another person with an umbrella, hold your umbrella higher if you can. Let the other person pass under your umbrella. But do not knock them in the head!

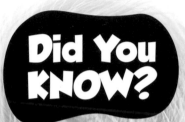

Did You KNOW?

Leave your wet umbrella at the door in Japan. In restaurants and stores, umbrella holders are by the door. It is rude to bring a wet umbrella inside.

Open your umbrella outside a bus or train. Shake it off before you walk inside. And never place your wet umbrella on an open seat. No one likes a soggy seat!

Being Clean

Make sure you wear clean clothes on a clean body. Take baths or showers as often as you need them. Get the dirt out from under your nails, too.

And don't wear your pepperoni on your sweater! Check your clothes before you step outside. Do they have stains or food on them? Do they smell like the gym?

People sitting or standing near you in public don't want to smell your stinky socks. Wear messy clothes and people will think you are a messy person.

Who's Next?

You need to wait in line at many places. You wait to pay for things at a store. At school, you wait in the lunch line. If you do not know where to stand, watch others. Stand behind them. Don't just push your way to the front. And never cut in front of others. It is not nice. You might knock the food off someone's tray.

Did You KNOW?

In England, waiting in line is called "queuing." People who cut in line are queue jumpers. And cutting in line is very rude to the English.

Do not stand too close to others. Give each person a bit of space. It is no fun when someone is breathing down your neck!

Remember to be **patient**. You will soon get to the front of the line.

Litter Bugs

It is fun to have picnics and eat outside. But do not leave your napkins and wrappers on the ground. No one likes to see **litter**. Just take a minute to find a trashcan. Leave parks and streets clean. You keep the space nice for others. Even little critters will be thankful. You help keep public spaces nice and **tidy** by not being a litter bug.

Your Seat

You found a great seat by the door on a bus. But check out the other people on the bus. Do any look like they need to sit more than you? A woman who is going to have a baby may have sore feet. Or it might be hard for an older person to stand. Offer your seat to someone who might need it. Stand up and ask, "Would you like to sit down?"

Say the Right Thing

It is nice when someone holds the door for you. Remember to say, "Thank you!"

If you bump into someone, say, "**Excuse** me" or "Sorry." They will know it was an **accident**. Saying sorry will turn a person's frown upside down.

It feels great when someone tells you to have a nice day. Tell that person, "Thanks, you too." A thank you can make another person's day a lot better.

A Bit More Polite

Remember to take care of public spaces. They are home to every person in the world. And animals share our public spaces, too.

Good manners in public keep everyone happy. They make life a little easier and nicer. So take a shower and pick up your trash. Give up your bus seat and turn down your music. And thank someone every day. Show respect to others. They will show respect to you, too.

Quick QUIZ

Put your new public manners in action with this pop quiz! Will you make the polite move?

You should always open your umbrella:

a. inside the house.
b. on a bus or a train.
c. outside a bus or train.
d. when it is not raining at all.

When waiting in line, you should:

a. sit down on the floor and cry.
b. stand very close to the person in front of you.
c. be patient.
d. jump to the front of the line.

When you are at a picnic, you should:

a. play catch with your trash.
b. dump everything on the ground and leave.
c. put trash in a trashcan.
d. neatly pile your trash on the grass.

When you are riding on a bus or a train, a good person to give your seat to is:

a. Spider-man.

b. a dog.

c. Elvis Presley.

d. an older person.

If you bump into someone, say:

a. "Get out of my way!"

b. "Excuse me."

c. "Watch it!"

d. "Hurry up, you turtle!"

Glossary

accident (AK-si-duhnt): An accident is something that happens without being planned and may end up with someone being hurt. Chris bumped into Max by accident.

excuse (ek-SKYOOZ): To excuse someone is to forgive the person for doing something. "Excuse me for stepping on your toe!"

litter (LIT-ur): Litter is garbage that people toss on the ground or in the water. Do not throw litter on the ground.

patient (PAY-shuhnt): A patient person can deal with problems or waiting without getting mad. Be patient when you wait in line.

polite (puh-LITE): To be polite is to have good manners. It is polite to be quiet at a movie.

respect (ri-SPEKT): To have respect is to care for another person's feelings or treat his or her home with care. Turn your music down to show respect to others.

tidy (TYE-dee): A tidy space is neat and in order. A tidy park is good for everyone.

Web Sites

Visit our Web site for links about manners in public: **childsworld.com/links**

Note to Parents, Teachers, and Librarians: We routinely verify our Web links to make sure they are safe and active sites. So encourage your readers to check them out!

Books

Burstein, John. *Manners, Please!: Why It Pays to be Polite.* New York: Crabtree, 2011.

Eberly, Sheryl. *365 Manners Kids Should Know: Games, Activities, and Other Fun Ways to Help Children Learn Etiquette.* New York: Three Rivers Press, 2001.

Espeland, Pamela. *Dude, That's Rude!* Minneapolis, MN: Free Spirit Publishing, 2007.

Index